Matchstick Dreams

A Play

Fiz Marcus

A Samuel French Acting Edition

SAMUELFRENCH-LONDON.CO.UK
SAMUELFRENCH.COM

Copyright © 1999 by Fiz Marcus
All Rights Reserved

MATCHSTICK DREAMS is fully protected under the copyright laws of the British Commonwealth, including Canada, the United States of America, and all other countries of the Copyright Union. All rights, including professional and amateur stage productions, recitation, lecturing, public reading, motion picture, radio broadcasting, television and the rights of translation into foreign languages are strictly reserved.

ISBN 978-0-573-12157-9

www.samuelfrench-london.co.uk

www.samuelfrench.com

FOR AMATEUR PRODUCTION ENQUIRIES

UNITED KINGDOM AND WORLD
EXCLUDING NORTH AMERICA
plays@SamuelFrench-London.co.uk
020 7255 4302/01

Each title is subject to availability from Samuel French,
depending upon country of performance.

CAUTION: Professional and amateur producers are hereby warned that MATCHSTICK DREAMS is subject to a licensing fee. Publication of this play does not imply availability for performance. Both amateurs and professionals considering a production are strongly advised to apply to the appropriate agent before starting rehearsals, advertising, or booking a theatre. A licensing fee must be paid whether the title is presented for charity or gain and whether or not admission is charged.

The professional rights in this play are controlled by Samuel French Ltd, 52 Fitzroy Street, London, W1T 5JR.

No one shall make any changes in this title for the purpose of production. No part of this book may be reproduced, stored in a retrieval system, or transmitted in any form, by any means, now known or yet to be invented, including mechanical, electronic, photocopying, recording, videotaping, or otherwise, without the prior written permission of the publisher. No one shall upload this title, or part of this title, to any social media websites.

The right of Fiz Marcus to be identified as author of this work has been asserted by her in accordance with Section 77 of the Copyright, Designs and Patents Act 1988

CHARACTERS

George Balmforth: mid 60s
Dora Balmforth: mid 60s
Delivery Man
Stan: late 50s

The roles of **Stan** and the **Delivery Man** can be played by the same actor

Note: All characters are Leeds born and bred

The action of the play takes place in the living-room of the Balmforths' suburban semi-detached house in Leeds

SYNOPSIS OF SCENES

Scene 1	Late autumn; five p.m.
Scene 2	Two hours later
Scene 3	Two days later; early evening
Scene 4	Six months later; early afternoon

Time — the present

For
Mum and Dad

Other plays by Fiz Marcus published by Samuel French Ltd

As Fiz Coleman, with John Gardiner:

Bad Day at Black Frog Creek
Mr Macaroni and the Exploding Pizza Pie
The Snatching of Horrible Harold
Surgical Sensations at St Sennapod's

MATCHSTICK DREAMS

Scene 1

The living-room of a suburban semi-detached house in Leeds. Late autumn. About five o'clock in the evening

There are doors R and L, the R one leading to the hall, the L to the kitchen. There is a window R which looks out on to the street. At the back, C, there is a sideboard with two candlesticks and a bowl of silk flowers on it. DC is a sofa with a coffee table in front of it and a magazine rack with a catalogue in it at one end. There is a dining table L with about thirty matchboxes and a pile of newspaper clippings on it and two dining chairs beneath it

When the play begins, George, a man in his mid sixties, sits at the dining table L reading a newspaper clipping. Dora, his wife, also in her mid sixties, sits on the sofa reading the evening paper

Dora Would you credit it?
George Umm.
Dora He's got engaged.
George Who 'as?
Dora Paul.
George Who?
Dora Maureen Simpkins' youngest.
George Oh ay.
Dora He 'ad a speech impediment if I remember rightly. No, I tell a lie, that were 'is brother. It were 'im 'ad a squint. Or was it? Well, squint or stutter, someone's taken 'im.
George I allus said these matches 'd come in handy.

Dora What for?

George D'you know, there's some chap here has built Houses o' Parliament out of matches. I reckon I'll have a go at Town Hall.

Dora Wi' matches?

George Why not? Mind you it won't arf take a few. It says 'ere this chap used two 'undred and fifty thousand for Houses o' Parliament.

Dora Two 'undred and fifty thousand! You're daft, you are, George Balmforth, where are you going to get two 'undred and fifty thousand matches?

George I'll find 'em, never you mind.

Dora We've got no gas, we don't smoke, they ripped out fireplace and put in central heating fifteen years ago. The only matches we'll need is when we go up in smoke at crematorium.

George Don't talk morbid, woman.

Dora I'm facing facts, which is more than you're doing ... Two 'undred and fifty thousand matches! Think o' cost.

George It'll be worth a few bob when it's finished.

Dora What do you want for your tea? I got a bit of finnan haddock at Ramsey's, it'll poach nicely with an egg ... That do you?

George I'm easy.

Dora I bumped into Jeanna Crabshaw outside Kwik Save. Ooh, tinned tomatoes is cheap in there this week, we'd best pick up a couple of tins. She didn't look good.

George Who?

Dora Jeanna Crabshaw!

George Don't know her.

Dora Course you do, she's Minnie Thompson's younger sister, married Tommy Crabshaw, he worked at Pickering's.

George If you say so.

Dora I said to her, "How you feelin'?" "Not so good," she says, so I said to her, "No, you don't look it either." I'll go get on with that haddock. (*She puts down the paper and stands*)

George How many matches in a box?

Dora You're not still on about matches!

George It's good for me to 'ave a hobby. Doctor said so. Keeps your mind active.

Dora Why change the habitude of a lifetime at your age? It could be dangerous!

Scene 1

George 'Ere, what time is it?
Dora Just gone five: why?
George Oh — no reason, just wondered. Shouldn't you be getting on wi' tea?
Dora I were just going. Thought you weren't fussed.
George Ay, well I feel a bit peckish now.
Dora Clear all that rubbish off and set table, it'll be ready in about twenty minutes.

Dora exits L to the kitchen

George waits until Dora has closed the door, then goes quietly to the window and lifts the curtain to look out into the street. We hear the sound of a van pulling up outside and stopping

George Good lad!

The front doorbell rings

(*Calling out to Dora*) I'll get it, love!

George exits to the front door R

Dora (*off*) If it's canvassers for the election don't let 'em in. Just tell 'em we'll vote for whoever'll send a car for us.

George enters quietly, followed by a burly delivery man in overalls carrying three or four large cardboard boxes and his delivery note clipboard

Delivery Man Where do you want me to put 'em?
George (*whispering*) Ssh, keep your voice down.
Delivery Man What?
George It's the wife, she's feelin' poorly.
Delivery Man (*whispering*) Where do you want me to put 'em?
George (*looking around the room in some desperation*) Dunno. In 't sideboard?

Delivery Man You'll never get 'em in there. Look I can't 'ang about, they're not heavy. I'll leave 'em for you to sort out. Here's bill; it's seventy-four thirty-nine including VAT. (*He holds out his delivery note clipboard*) Sign here, please.
George (*signing the delivery note and taking money out of his wallet*) Here you are. Seventy-four forty. Keep the change.
Delivery Man Ta, mate. Ooh, I'll be out on 't town with that. Don't worry, I'll see meself out.

The Delivery Man exits

Dora (*off; calling*) Who was it, George?
George Er ... the Cleaneeze man, I told him we were all right.
Dora (*off*) Was it the one with the limp?
George Dunno, he was stood still.
Dora (*off*) I hardly think he were tap dancing. I hope you've set that table? It'll not be many minutes now.
George Yes, love.

George looks at the boxes, trying desperately to work out where to hide them. Finally, inspiration: he pushes the boxes underneath the coffee table in front of the sofa, goes to the top drawer of the sideboard, takes out a cloth and throws it over the table. From the top of the sideboard he takes the candlesticks and bowl of silk flowers and arranges them on the table; from the inside of the sideboard be takes knives, forks and serviettes and sets them on the table too. He takes a box of matches from the dining table and opens it, intending to light the candles. He looks at the matches in his hand

Blast, they're all spent!

He glances towards the kitchen door then gets down on his hands and knees and opens one of the boxes under the coffee table. He triumphantly withdraws a box of matches with which he lights the candles; then he turns off the main lights, stands back and surveys the scene

Champion!

Scene 1

Dora enters wheeling a trolley; on it are two plates of haddock and eggs, two glasses of water and a plate of bread and butter

Dora (*noticing the lights are off*) Oh drat it! Has the bulb gone again? Ooh, I shall give 'em what for. (*She notices the coffee table in all its splendour*) And what's this?
George Bulb's fine, love, I — er — thought we could 'ave a cosy candlelit tea; you know — er — just the two of us.
Dora George Balmforth you've gone soft in the 'ead. You can't eat at a coffee table.
George I thought it 'ud make a change.
Dora You'll drip egg all down your jumper, you mark my words. Oh, why waste my breath, get sat down or this'll be stone cold.

George sits on the sofa; Dora puts the plates down on the coffee table and sits. They begin to eat

George Very nice; I allus said you did a nice bit of finnan haddock. (*He indicates the candles*) Told you those matches would come in 'andy.
Dora Umm. I've never been one for eating wi' candles, it makes me nervous. You can't see what you're eating.
George But you know what you're eating; you made it.
Dora Well, you never know what might 'ave dropped in.
George (*puzzled*) What you talking about?
Dora 'Ave you forgot what Stan found in his dinner at that fancy French restaurant on Berwick Street?
George (*remembering with distaste*) No — but you're not likely to find a ——
Dora That'll do, I don't need reminding. (*Pause*). I 'ope it wasn't the one wi the limp.
George Eh?
Dora The Cleaneeze man, I allus order something from 'im ... I think they send 'em out deliberate, you know. So's you feel sorry for 'em and buy.
George 'Appen.
Dora (*finishing eating and picking up the corner of the cloth*) Nice cloth, this one, I got it in the sale at Lewis's, or was it the one your

Florrie gave us? Looks as though it could do with a wash. I'll pop it in on a delicates tonight.

George (*fearful that Dora might see the boxes*) I shouldn't bother with that, love. It looks fine to me, probably just the light. Didn't you say you fancied an early night? I'll put the blanket on and bring you up a tray of tea ... and — er — don't worry about the dishes, I'll do 'em.

Dora It's half-past five. What's got into you?

George Nowt... I just thought ...er ...

Dora I'm not going to bed at half past five.

George No, I don't suppose you are.

Silence; they both stare ahead

Dora Thought you were going to do the dishes.

George (*reluctant to leave her on her own*) I will soon.

Silence

'Ere, what day is it? It's not Bingo tonight, is it?

Dora No, Bingo's Thursdays. It's Tuesday. You collected the pensions this morning, 'ave you forgotten? Seventy-five pounds there should be.

George (*weakly*) Ay, there should be ...

Dora I shall need that tomorrow when we go to Kwik Save.

George We can't — it's closed — er — renovations.

Dora Since when? Oh well, it'll 'ave to be Morrison's then.

George I'm not feelin' so good, I might not be up to it.

Dora I knew there was something wrong wi' you. You've been acting most peculiar all night.

George 'Ave I?

Dora You're up to summat.

George Me?

Dora Well, I don't see anyone else here. I think you'd best come clean.

George (*swallowing nervously*) Well, you see, love ——

There is a loud banging on the back door which interrupts him

Scene 1

Dora Who'll that be?

George starts to rise, anxious to escape

Oh, no, you don't. I'll get it.

Dora exits into the kitchen

(*Calling as she goes*) 'Ang on, 'ang on!
George Oh, Hamlet, now what!
Dora (*off*) There's no need to break down door.

We hear the sound of the door opening

Oh, it's only you, is it, what's all bangin' about? George, it's Stan. Well go on, you'd best go through. How's your mam?

Dora enters the room followed by Stan, a very thin tall man with receding hair and glasses, in his late fifties. He shifts awkwardly from foot to foot, obviously a man uncomfortable with his body

Stan Not so hot; her legs is bad, she thinks it's the cold weather. Hallo George, sorry to interrupt your tea.
Dora We've done.
Stan Celebration, eh? (*He indicates the candles*)
George No — er ——
Dora Oh, for heaven's sake blow out them candles while I switch on 't light; it puts me in mind of a funeral parlour ... (*She puts on the light*)

George reluctantly blows out the candles

Don't just stand there, Stan, 'ave a seat.
Stan (*sitting*) Ta, I won't stay; just wanted to have a word wi' George.
Dora You're not the only one. (*To George*) Don't think I've forgot, we've got unfinished business you and me.
George Yes, love.

Dora I'll leave you to it, I'll be in 't kitchen and don't forget to clear them plates.

Dora exits to the kitchen

George No, love. (*He waits until Dora has gone and turns urgently to Stan*) By 'eck, I'm glad to see you.
Stan Why?
George They've come.
Stan Will you be eating that bread?
George What?
Stan The bread. (*He indicates the plate of bread and butter*) Only what with Mam's legs I haven't 'ad mi tea yet and I could do with ——
George (*impatiently*) Take it; go on.

Stan leans forward and takes a piece of bread which he folds in two and begins to munch with obvious pleasure

I said they've come.
Stan Your matches?
George Of course, what do you think I mean?
Stan Where are they?
George (*lifting the edge of the tablecloth*) There! But they can't stay there, there'll be merry hell to pay if Dora finds them ... I need your help; can you take 'em?
Stan I don't know as I can, me back's been playin up.
George Stan, we're talking about boxes of matches, not crates of bitter.
Stan Well, mebbe ...
George There's no mebbe about it; if them boxes isn't out of here before Dora comes back, my life won't be worth livin'.
Dora (*off, calling from the kitchen*) You started to load that trolley yet?
George (*calling*) I'm on me way, love. (*To Stan, urgently*) Look here, just take 'em out front door ...

Scene 1

Stan And then what?

George Put em in the shed at the allotment, and I'll bring 'em back as I need them.

Stan It seems a bit of a performance, can't you just tell 'er; I mean — they're only matches.

George Will you just do as I ask you? I haven't been married to Dora for forty-five years for nothing.

Stan All right, but don't blame me if they get damp. (*He gets down on his hands and knees and begins to take a box out from under the table*)

George Damp is the least of my problems, when she finds out where the pension money's gone ...

The phone in the hall rings, and they both freeze

Dora (*calling from the kitchen*) Leave it, it'll be for me!

Dora enters, wiping her hands on a tea towel. She sees Stan on his hands and knees

What the ... ?

George He's looking for his contact lens, aren't you Stan?

Stan I don't ——

George You better get that phone!

Dora exits to the hall

Dora (*off*) You're worse than a couple kids, you two!

We hear Dora pick up the phone

Hallo, 687421 ... Oh, hallo June, I thought it might be you. ... How is he?

George That were close!

Dora (*on the phone*) Oh dear, I am sorry to hear that. But they can do marvellous things these days. You mustn't sit there brooding.

Stan But I don't wear contact lenses.

George How's she to know ?

Stan I'm wearing me glasses!
Dora (*off*) How long will they keep him in? ... The end of the week, he must be bad.
George Well, take 'em off!
Stan I can't see a thing without them.
Dora (*off*) Oh, June, don't take on so. I know it's hard ... Look I've got that catalogue you were asking about; what if I pop over for an hour or so and we can look through it? Take your mind off things.
George Just take 'em off! Sit here on 't sofa and keep your mouth shut.

Stan takes off his glasses and puts them in his pocket; he sits gingerly on the sofa

Dora (*off*) No, it's no trouble; I'll see you in ten minutes. ... Bye.

We hear Dora hang up the phone

Dora enters

Ooh poor June, she's in a shocking state.
George I thought Harry was looking a bit off colour last week.
Dora Harry? He's all right, it's Billy.
George Who?
Dora The budgie!
Stan I had a budgie once, it ——
George All right, Stan ... So you'll be going round there, then?
Dora I'll not be long. Stan, pass us that catalogue in the rack beside you.

Stan feels his way to the end of the settee, obviously unable to focus on anything

What's up with him?
George Er — I told you, he's having trouble with his contact lenses. Here, I'll get it ... (*He picks up the catalogue during the following*)

Scene 1

Dora I could've sworn you were wearing glasses when you came in.
Stan I'm — er ——
George He's just trying 'em out.
Dora Well, I'd get back to glasses if I were you — and there's nowt wrong with my eyes, George Balmforth; those tea things is still sitting there.
George (*handing Dora the catalogue*) I'll clear 'em, I said I would; you get off to June's, eh? Shall I fetch your coat?
Dora I can manage, it's in the hall. You are up to something. It's no good trying to look innocent, I know you too well. Whatever it is I'll find out. Don't worry. 'Night, Stan.
Stan 'Night, Mrs Balmforth.
Dora (*to George; ominously*) I'll see you later .

Dora exits to the hall

We hear the front door slam

George (*sitting down on the sofa wth relief*) Oh Stan, I'm not cut out for this!
Stan (*putting his glasses on*) Are you sure it's worth the bother? Why don't you just take the matches back and forget about it. If you want summat to do why not come fishing with me or spend more time at the allotment?
George You don't understand, I can't.
Stan I'm sure they'd give you your money back.
George I said you'd not understand. Dora won't either. It's important to me this, the most important thing I've ever done. I'm sixty-four years old; I've never done anything I've been really proud of. I want — I want to leave me mark, create something that's never been done before.
Stan I can see what you're getting at, but maybe you should start with something a bit smaller, less ambitious.
George No it has to be Leeds Town Hall! And I've made me mind up, I've had enough of this shilly-shallying; I shall tell Dora and if she doesn't like it she can lump it!

Stan I think you're mebbe being a bit hasty, George; I mean you said yourself that Dora ... Well, you know.

George That Dora what? That Dora wears the trousers? Well maybe after forty-five years I'm tired of wearing a skirt. Perhaps you ought to think about it too!

Stan (*taking off his glasses and polishing them with a handkerchief*) That were uncalled for.

George I'm sorry.

Stan (*standing*) I'd best be getting back. You'll not be needing me to shift these boxes, then?

George Don't go off in a huff, Stan, it's just that I've been thinking recently.

Stan So I see.

George I can't explain it.

Stan Thought we were mates.

George Course we are. Here, I'm gonna need a mate when I tell Dora. You'll be able to hear the ructions from here to Bradford.

Stan Rather you than me. I'd best be off, me mam'll think I've got lost. I said I'd only be five minutes.

George Do you fancy a swift half down the road? I could do with a bit of dutch courage.

Stan I shouldn't ... Oh what the 'eck, why not!

George Good lad! I'll get me jacket.

George exits to the hall

Stan What about these dishes?

George (*off; calling from the hall*) They can wait! Come on!

Stan looks around the room and then exits to the hall

We hear the front door open and then slam shut

Black-out

Scene 2

The same. Two hours later

The dishes from tea are still on the table. Dora is sitting on the sofa leafing through the catalogue she has brought back with her. She is obviously passing time until George returns

We hear a key turning in the front door, then the door opening and shutting. Dora closes the catalogue and sits with her arms crossed

George enters

George Bit nippy out there. How's June?
Dora Where've you been? I've been worried sick.
George I popped out for a half with Stan.
Dora Anything could've 'appened to you.
George I've only been to the end of the road.
Dora You could eve been lying senseless in the gutter.
George On a half of bitter?
Dora Don't get clever with me, you know what I'm talking about. I came back, found the tea things just as I'd left them, lights blazing away, I thought there'd been an emergency. You never think, that's your problem.
George No love, sorry.
Dora That or you're going senile. I can't trust you to do anything these days; you said you'd do the dishes and they're still here. This place is like a pigsty. You leave things all over the place — look at that table. (*She indicates the dining table*) You're forever snipping things out of the paper. You'll never use them; it's just more clutter, and who has to clear up after you? Me! It's worse than when our Joan was small, having you around all day.
George Dora, will you just calm down a minute — and can we talk?
Dora Talk? What do you think I've just been doing? Talking's not going to clear this room, is it?
George Will you listen to me for a minute?
Dora (*clearing the dishes off the coffee table and putting them on the trolley*) I haven't got time to listen, I s'pose I'll have to clear

away as usual and pop this cloth in the machine. (*She removes the cloth from the table and reveals the boxes*)

George Oh, Hamlet!

Dora What the blazes are these?

George I've been trying to tell you, they're matches.

Dora All of them? Are you planning on becoming a pyromaniac?

George They're for me model.

Dora You really have gone senile.

George I am going to build a model of Leeds Town Hall out of matches; is that clear enough for you?

Dora You must be mad!

George It might be the last thing I'll ever do, but mark my words I'll do it.

Dora Why?

George Because I want to.

Dora We all want things, it doesn't mean we get them.

George No, but this is something I *can* do, for me.

Dora This is ridiculous! What will the neighbours say?

George They can say what they want, it doesn't bother me.

Dora Where did the money come from?

George I — er — borrowed it.

Dora Who from?

George This week's pension. I'll pay it back. I've still got some of my redundancy money left.

Dora I don't believe I'm hearing this. You've spent seventy-five pounds on matches!

George Seventy-four forty. All I'll need now is the glue. And mebbe a couple of books, but I can always get them from the library.

Dora And where do you propose building it?

George Here.

Dora Oh no!

George Why not?

Dora This is a sitting-room, not a workshop; think of the carpet.

George What about it?

Dora It's an eighty-twenty twist pile from Kingsway. I'm not having glue trod in it.

George I'll be careful, I'll put down paper.
Dora Who's put you up to this?
George No-one, it's my idea and you'll not stop me.
Dora You need locking up. I shall ring our Joan, see if she can talk some sense into you.
George Why? It's nowt to do with her.
Dora It's not normal.
George I've been normal for sixty-four years and look where it's got me.
Dora Thank you very much. It's nice to know I'm appreciated.
George Oh Dora, don't you see, there has to be more to life than Kwik Save and finnan haddock and eighty-twenty twist pile!
Dora I'm not listening to any more of this nonsense, I'm going to bed. I want those matches out of here by tomorrow morning.
George I'm sorry Dora. I won't change me mind.
Dora We'll see about that!

Dora gathers her things together and sweeps out into the hall

George (*sitting down on the sofa*) Oh — Bubbles!

Black-out

Scene 3

The same. Two days later. Early evening

There is an air of disorder about the room with newspapers on chairs, plates and cups scattered around. On the table there is now a large pot of glue, the beginnings of a slightly lopsided construction made from matches, piles of matches and matchboxes, plans and diagrams and a number of large books

George sits at the table in front of the construction

There is a banging at the back door

George It's open, come in!

Stan enters from the kitchen

Stan It's only me. I just wondered how it was going.
George Well, what do you think?
Stan Very nice.
George Is that all you can say?
Stan Did you change your mind, then?
George What are you talking about? Of course I didn't change me mind, I'm building it, aren't I?
Stan I can see that, I meant did you change your mind about Leeds Town Hall?
George No, why?
Stan Oh, maybe it's me eyes then, it's just that I thought it were the Leaning Tower of Pisa.
George Ay well, mebbe it is a bit lopsided, but I can soon fix that. It's not easy, you know.
Stan I can imagine. (*He looks around the room*) She's not back then?
George No, but I can manage. I'm not entirely helpless.
Stan She'll go spare when she sees this place, all them papers and plates.
George I'll clear 'em all in good time; the world won't come to an end just because there's a few things lying around.
Stan I don't mind giving you a hand. I've got ten minutes before tea.
George I don't think so, Stan, I can't be distracted at the moment; this is a very delicate operation. Thanks all the same.
Stan Right, I'll be off then. Just thought I'd check you were all right. I mean, if you fancied a bit of company you know you can always pop next door.
George I'm fine, don't you worry about me. To tell you the truth I'm enjoying the peace and quiet.
Stan I s'pose you would.
George How's your mam?
Stan Fair to middlin'. Mustn't complain, she's got some new ——

Scene 3

We hear the sound of a key turning in the front door

Oh 'eck, is that Dora?
George Well, unless it's a burglar with a key, I should think it is.
Stan I'd best be off. (*He turns to leave*)

Dora enters carrying a small suitcase. She totally ignores George and addresses everything to Stan

George Hallo, love, did you have a nice break?
Dora Hallo, Stan. Oh, I don't know what they think they're playing at with the buses, I've had to wait twenty minutes at the station for a number thirty-six and not a word of apology. I asked the conductor what was going on. "Rationalization," he says. "What's that when it's at home?" I said. That stumped him. Oh, I could murder a cup of tea; I wasn't paying British Rail prices, or whatever they are now that they're privatized. Would you like one, Stan? I'll pop the kettle on.
Stan No thanks, Mrs Balmforth, I'm just about to have me tea.
George I'll join you, love.
Dora Right, just me then.

Dora exits to the kitchen and carries on the conversation from there

George How's our Joan and the children?
Dora (*off*) Joan sends her love, Stan.
Stan (*looking at George in bewilderment*) Oh, ta, how is she?
Dora (*off*) Fine, she's got her hands full on her own with those kids though.
Stan I expect she has.
Dora (*off*) That Susan is a right little madam and only seven, wants to be a Spice Girl if you don't mind, and all Andrew thinks about is football and videos. It wasn't like that in our day.
Stan No.

Silence

George Are there any clean cups, love? I would have cleared up before you got back but I didn't know when to expect you. You should've rung. I'd 'ave met you in and bought something for tea … (*He trails off*)

Dora appears in the doorway

Dora Stan, will you tell him that there is one clean cup, this place is a disgrace, but then that's all I would have expected from him. Furthermore, I have no intention of cooking, cleaning or washing for him, or communicating directly with him, until he comes to his senses. I trust I've made myself clear.
Stan She says that there ——
George All right, Stan, I heard.
Dora Oh and from now on I shall be sleeping in the spare room.
Stan From now on ——
George Stan! I am not deaf!
Stan (*backing his way out of the room towards the back door*) No, right — er — I'll be off. I'll see you soon, George. Good-night, Mrs Balmforth.
Dora 'Night, Stan, give my regards to your mam.
Stan Right.

Stan exits. We hear the back door slam

Dora exits to the kitchen and returns with a cup of tea. She sits down on the sofa and begins to look at the paper, studiously ignoring George. Silence

George Come on, Dora, this is ridiculous, you can't carry on like this. You're the one who needs to come to your senses, not me.

No response

Look, love, what I'm doing, it's not worth all this. I'm not doing it deliberately to upset you, it's just something that I want to do. No, not want, need to do. Surely after forty-five years of marriage

Scene 3

I'm entitled to do one thing just for meself. How much longer have we got together, you and I? Ten years, maybe twenty years if we're lucky. I know you don't like talking about it, but we've got to face facts; we don't know what's going to happen — I could drop dead tomorrow. We should be trying to make the most of the time, not trying to make each other's lives a misery. I know I'm not perfect, we neither of us is, but we've made it this far and that must count for something. (*Pause*) Look, suppose we were to try to build it together? I've got to admit, it's a bit more tricky than I thought it would be, and you used to be a dab hand at making things. Remember that elephant you made for our Joan?
Dora (*quietly*) Donkey.
George Eh?
Dora It were a donkey, and I knitted it.
George Well, you still made it.

Silence

Dora Will cheese on toast do you for your tea? I don't expect you've been to Kwik Save.
George Cheese on toast'd be champion, if it's not too much trouble. I'll take your case up shall I? (*Pause*) Where shall I put it?
Dora Where do you think? (*Pause*) In our room of course!
George Of course.

George exits with the case, heading upstairs

Dora heads for the kitchen, stopping on the way to look at the model

Dora That's never Leeds Town Hall!

Dora exits

The Lights fade to Black-out

Scene 4

The same. Six months later. Early afternoon

The table is cleared of all the matches, books and the model, and the room has returned to its habitual neatness

A knock is heard at the back door. We hear the back door open

Stan enters the room dressed in a smart dark suit with the sleeves and trousers a little short. He is obviously dressed in his best suit. His hair is slicked back

Stan (*calling*) Hallo, George?
George (*off; calling from upstairs*) I'm upstairs.
Stan You ready? I've brought the car round to 't front; we'd best be getting off.
George With you in a second, Stan.
Stan You don't want to be late, do you?
George We've plenty of time.
Stan You never know with traffic.
George Don't fuss.

George enters the room dressed in a shirt, tie and suit

Stan I'd never forgive meself if you were late, you having trusted me an' all.
George All right, Stan, there's no need to get carried away.
Stan It's not everyday you get presented to the Mayor of Leeds.
George Where is that woman? She'll be late for her own funeral. (*Calling*) Dora, get a move on, Stan's waiting!
Dora I'm coming.
Stan Have you got the invitation?
George In my pocket, but I shouldn't think we'll need it.
Stan No, I expect they'll recognize you both, you having had your pictures in 't paper. Me mam was so chuffed she's had it framed and put on 't wall next to me City and Guilds.

Scene 4

George *That's nice. (Calling) Dora, come on!*
Stan Is the model in 't library already?
George They collected it last week. This is just the formal handing over.
Stan Well, you did it, George. I never thought you would, but you did.
George It wasn't just me, Stan — I couldn't have done it without Dora.
Stan No, she really come up trumps.
George Did she tell you we're thinking about tackling the Taj Mahal next?
Stan Ooh, that'll take some doing.
George I think we'll manage. (*He looks at his watch*) What is she doing up there? We shall be late if she doesn't look out.
Stan It'll be quite a do, I expect. Will they be laying on tea?
George I don't know, Stan. (*Calling*) Dora, we haven't got all day!

Dora comes into the room smartly dressed in a suit and wearing a hat and gloves

Dora Don't rush me, I'm not going out in a panic, this is a special occasion and I want to look right. Is this hat straight?
Stan You look a right bobby-dazzler, Mrs Balmforth.
Dora Thanks, Stan.
George You look champion, love; now can we go?
Dora Let me look at you. (*She flicks an imaginary bit of fluff off George's jacket*) There! You don't look so bad yourself. Come on then, what are we waiting for? To the Central Library please, Stan.

They all exit into the hall

We hear the front door slam and the sound of a car starting up

The Lights fade to Black-out

FURNITURE AND PROPERTY LIST

Scene 1

On stage: Sideboard. *In it*: tablecloth, knives and forks, serviettes. *On it* : two candlesticks with candles, bowl of silk flowers.
Sofa. *On it*: evening newspaper for **Dora**
Small dining table. *On it*: boxes of used matches, newspaper clippings
Magazine rack. *In it*: catalogue
Two dining chairs
Coffee table

Off stage: Three or four large cardboard boxes one of which contains at least one box of live matches; clipboard and delivery note (**Delivery Man**)
Trolley. *On it*: two plates of haddock and eggs, two glasses of water, plate of bread and butter (**Dora**)
Tea towel (**Dora**)

Personal: **George:** wallet/purse containing notes and coins; watch (worn throughout)
Dora: watch (worn throughout)
Stan: glasses (worn throughout), handkerchief

Scene 2

Set: Catalogue on sofa for **Dora**

Furniture and Property List

Scene 3

Set: Newspapers, dirty plates, cups and saucers.
Large pot of glue and brush
Matchstick construction
Matches and matchboxes
Diagrams and plans
Books

Strike: Trolley

Off stage: Small suitcase (**Dora**)
Cup of tea (**Dora**)

LIGHTING PLOT

Property fittings required: nil
One interior with exterior backing. The same scene throughout.

S CENE 1

To open: General interior lighting

Cue 1	**George** switches off main light *Cut main lights; bring up covering spots on candles*	(Page 4)
Cue 2	**Dora** puts on main light *Bring up general interior lighting; cut covering spots*	(Page 7)
Cue 3	The front door slams shut *Black-out*	(Page 12)

S CENE 2

To open: General interior lighting

Cue 4	**George:** "Oh — Bubbles." *Black-out*	(Page 15)

S CENE 3

To open: General interior lighting

Cue 5	**Dora** "That's never Leeds Town Hall!" *Fade to black-out*	(Page 19)

Lighting Plot

Scene 4

To open: General interior lighting with early spring afternoon effect on exterior backing

Cue 6   The front door slams and the car starts up   (Page 21)
Fade to black-out

EFFECTS PLOT

Cue 1	**George** lifts the curtain *Van drawing up and stopping*	(Page 3)
Cue 2	**George:** "Good lad!" *Front doorbell rings*	(Page 3)
Cue 3	**Delivery Man:** " ... I'll see meself out." He exits *Front door slams*	(Page 4)
Cue 4	**George:** "Well you see, love ——" *Banging on back door*	(Page 6)
Cue 5	**Dora** (*off*): " ... to break down door." *Back door opens*	(Page 7)
Cue 6	**George:** " ... where the pension money's gone ... " *Telephone rings*	(Page 9)
Cue 7	**Dora:** "I'll see you later." She exits *Front door opens and then slams*	(Page 11)
Cue 8	**Stan** exits to the hall *Front door opens and then slams*	(Page 12)
Cue 9	Opening of SCENE 2: when ready *Sound of key in lock and front door opening and closing*	(Page 13)
Cue 10	Opening of SCENE 3: when ready *Banging on back door*	(Page 15)
Cue 11	**Stan**: " ... complain, she's got some new —— " *Sound of key in lock and front door opening and closing*	(Page 16)

Effects Plot

Cue 12   **Stan** exits (Page 18)
Back door slams

Cue 13   To open SCENE 4 *(Page 19)*
Knock at back door; sound of back door opening

Cue 14   **George**, **Dora** and **Stan** exit (Page 21)
Front door slams, followed by sound of car starting up and moving off

www.ingramcontent.com/pod-product-compliance
Lightning Source LLC
Chambersburg PA
CBHW070455050426
42450CB00012B/3283